Obesity

The Child's World

Published by The Child's World®
1980 Lookout Drive • Mankato, MN 56003-1705
800-599-READ • www.childsworld.com

Acknowledgments
The Child's World®: Mary Berendes, Publishing Director
Red Line Editorial: Editorial direction
The Design Lab: Design
Amnet: Production
Photographs ©: Front cover: Jaimie Duplass/Shutterstock Images;
Pixelbliss/Shutterstock Images; FoodIcons; FoodIcons, 3, 21; Kids
in Motion, 4, 6, 11, 19; ClarkandCompany/iStockphoto, 5; Hong
Vo/Shutterstock Images, 7; Pixelbliss/Shutterstock Images, 8;
Bikeriderlondon/Shutterstock Images, 9; Jaimie Duplass/Shutterstock
Images, 10; BrandX Images, 12, 18, 23; Thomas_EyeDesign/
iStockphoto, 13; PhotoDisc, 14; ComStock, 16

ISBN: 978-1623235383
LCCN: 2013931339

Printed in the United States of America
Mankato, MN
July, 2013
PA02174

ABOUT THE AUTHOR

Christie Rose Ritter is an award-winning journalist who has researched and written about government, education, science, nature, health, and business for newspapers, magazines, and web sites. Ritter has a bachelor's degree in political science from the University of California–Los Angeles and a master's degree in mass communications from San Diego State University. She's the proud mother of Vienna, who loves reading, and Kellen, who loves writing.

Table of Contents

What Is Obesity?

"Hey, guys, wait up!" It's no fun to be the slowest one heading out for recess. When kids have extra pounds on their bodies, it is harder to keep up. Running, skipping, and jumping are fun things to do, but it is not easy for children whose bodies are loaded with too many pounds.

People need to move to stay healthy. A hundred years ago, Americans were much more active. Children had to walk to school. Adults had to walk to work or to the train station if they had a job far away. People stayed healthy and fit by walking,

working on their farms, and doing daily chores.

Today, most children ride in a car or bus to school. Kids spend more time in front of a screen. They watch TV, play computer games, or use other electronics. Kids do not move enough when they do these activities, so they do not burn **calories**. Calories are what kids use to get energy. When they do not burn enough calories by staying active, unused calories get stored as **fat**.

When people eat more calories than they burn off through activity, they have a higher chance of becoming **overweight** or **obese**. When people are overweight, they weigh more and have more fat than they

▼ *Staying active helps you burn calories and avoid becoming overweight.*

FOOD IN SCHOOLS

What's on the lunch menu at school? Cheesy pizza? Chicken fingers and fries? Chocolate milk? Some schools have vending machines where kids can buy soda, chips, and candy. None of these items contains fresh vegetables or fruit. These are very tempting and might be tasty, but they are not healthy choices. Some school lunch menus now offer more healthy items such as salad bars and vegetarian meals.

should for their height. It is not healthy for our bodies to carry around too many pounds. When someone is very overweight, they are considered obese. Obesity is a serious problem in the United States. About one out of every three kids in the United States is overweight or obese.

▶ *Pizza is not a healthy meal choice.*

CHAPTER TWO

Why Is Obesity Unhealthy?

The children in the United States today could be the first to have shorter lives than their parents. Obese children have a very high chance of becoming obese adults. Doctors and health experts want to stop obesity during childhood. They believe the problem gets worse as people get older. The more a person weighs, the harder it is to become a healthy weight.

Children who are overweight or obese are at risk for several different health issues. Obese kids may get type 2 **diabetes**. Type 2

▲ *Fatty foods are tasty but can lead to obesity.*

▶ *Opposite page: Being obese as a child can lead to health problems as a grown-up.*

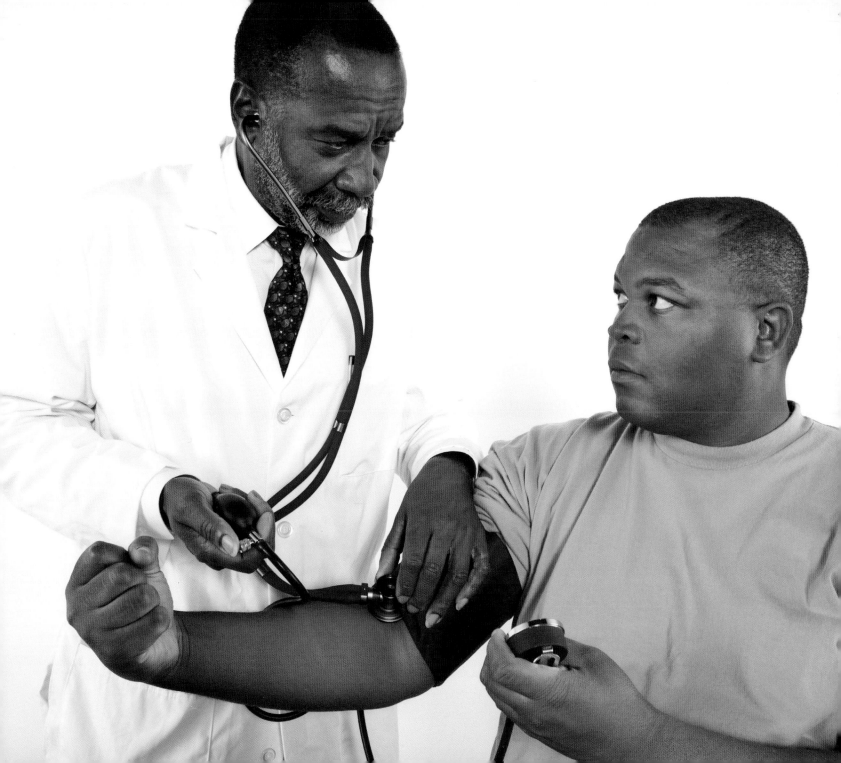

diabetes is a disease that makes it difficult for the body to manage its sugar levels. Obesity can also cause high blood pressure. High blood pressure can lead to **heart disease**. If they last into adulthood, both of these diseases can shorten someone's life.

Obesity can affect someone's quality of life, too. Children who are overweight or obese often suffer from low **self-esteem**, especially when they are targeted by bullies. Self-esteem means having respect for yourself and your abilities. When kids have low self-esteem, they may not have a lot of respect for themselves.

Additionally, feeling stressed by being overweight or obese can cause

▼ *It can be difficult to have high self-esteem when you weigh more than you should.*

kids to do poorly in school. Sometimes, kids who are overweight or obese can feel so bad about themselves that they become depressed, or very sad. When someone feels depressed, he or she can lose interest in activities that used to be enjoyable, including going to school and hanging out with friends.

While obesity can cause serious health problems, many of these problems go away when someone loses the extra weight. Eating more fruits and vegetables and less fatty foods help get someone on the track toward weight loss. Getting more physical activity, such as playing tag or taking a hike, can also help someone lose weight.

▲ *Being physically active with a friend can help obese kids lose weight and avoid health issues.*

CHAPTER THREE

Staying Healthy Means Eating Right

Food fuels your body. When you do not eat for a long time, you probably feel hungry and tired. Healthy foods also give you important **nutrients** that help you grow. Eating fruits and vegetables gives your body the **vitamins** and **minerals** it needs to be strong and healthy. **Protein** builds strong muscles and bones.

   If you load your body with fattening foods such as chips, soda, and candy, you will feel hungry again soon. That is because these foods do not have

▲ *Blueberries are a healthy and sweet snack full of vitamins and minerals.*

the nutrients you need. Instead, these foods contain empty calories. That is why they are called *junk foods*. That means they do not give you the nutrients you need to be healthy; rather, they just give you lots of calories. Remember, eating more calories than the body can use is what makes people gain weight.

Instead, choose healthy foods full of vitamins, minerals, and protein. Start by eating a healthy

▶ *Choose colorful, healthy snacks such as strawberries over junk foods such as candy.*

breakfast. Filling up with nutritious foods early in the day prevents hunger. Smart breakfast choices include a bowl of cereal that is low in sugar and served with skim milk or a bowl of oatmeal topped with shredded apples and walnuts. For a healthy lunch or dinner, choose a lean protein, such as chicken or beans, and add a few vegetables and a glass of milk.

Do not forget to make healthy choices at snack time, too. It is hard to resist packages with cartoon characters on them. But what looks cool on the outside is not always a healthy choice. Lots of snack foods, such as doughnuts or cookies, are full of empty calories. Instead, choose fruits or vegetables, cereal bars, or a handful of nuts.

Drinking plenty of water is also important for a healthy you. It's tempting to choose a soda,

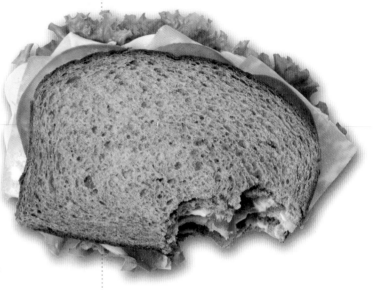

▲ *This sandwich, with healthy lunch meat and vegetables on whole wheat bread, is a healthy lunchtime meal.*

lemonade, or fruit punch, but these are loaded with sugar and calories. However, water does not have any calories. Fruit juice is full of good nutrients but has a lot of sugar. That makes fruit juice a once-in-a-while drink. Chocolate milk is another sweet drink that is an okay treat. Most of the time, though, make the healthy choice your body needs most: water.

Have you ever heard of the saying, "My eyes are bigger than my stomach"? Sometimes, tempting foods look so good that we eat way too much of them. Instead, start your meal with something healthy. Soup, salad, or cooked vegetables are great choices. Still hungry? Then, it is fine to have more. Start with small portion sizes. Eat slowly and listen to your body. Stop when you are full. Do not keep eating because the food looks good. Eat with your stomach, not your eyes!

CHAPTER FOUR

Staying Healthy Means Being Active

▼ *Many students play team sports such as baseball in gym class.*

How many minutes do you spend moving every day? Health experts say kids should move 60 minutes every day. If you are not moving for an hour each day, your chances of being overweight go up. Most kids get exercise in school. They play sports and games in gym class and at recess.

However, not all schools have these times for exercise. If your school does not have gym class or recess, try to spend a few minutes being active before school or during lunch. After school is a good time to move. Walking home with a parent is a great way to get some of your daily exercise. Or you can ask your parents to sign you up for an after-school exercise or sports program.

It is not easy to play outside if you live in a place that has cold winters or where it rains a lot. Instead, try a dance, karate, or gymnastics class. At home, have a jumping jack contest, skip rope, dance, or climb the stairs for exercise.

Whether it is wintertime or summertime, stay active by trying something new. It might be scary at first to join a sports team, but it is a great chance to make friends, get some exercise, and learn new skills. If you have tried softball and did not like it, maybe soccer is more your style. If team sports do not interest you, try something you can do on your own. Sports such as ice-skating or tae kwon do can be fun to do by yourself.

Is there a big traffic jam in the drop-off zone at your school? If your school offers a walk-to-school day, join the group. Or organize your neighborhood into a walking school bus. A walking school bus is a small group of kids who walk to school led by two or more parents. The parents take turns leading the group of kids in a walk to or from school.

◄ *Opposite page: Playing basketball is a great way to stay active over the winter.*

► *Martial arts such as karate or tae kwon do are fun to do by yourself.*

It is important to remember that being overweight or obese is something people can change. Eating right and getting lots of exercise are good first steps. Eat more fruits, vegetables, and proteins. Exercise for at least 60 minutes on most days. Don't be afraid to get started. Ask your parents to make a plan so the whole family can be at a healthy weight for life.

Hands-on Activity: A Visit to the Farmers' Market

Farmers' markets are popping up at schools, shopping malls, and city centers. If you live near one, plan a family outing that will end in a delicious meal!

What You'll Need:

your family, reusable bags

Directions:

1. First, grab your parents and get moving. Walk to the market if it is not too far away. Be sure to bring some reusable bags to fill.

2. Next, walk up and down the aisles to see which fruits and vegetables are in season. Talk over the selection with your parents. What type of meal could you make from the ingredients you see?

3. Then, buy your fresh fruits and vegetables and take them home to prepare. Help with cleaning, mixing, or measuring ingredients.

4. Sit down with your family to enjoy your healthy meal together. During dinner, talk about what you'll buy on your next trip to the farmers' market.

THE FARMERS' MARKET

Glossary

calories (KAL-ur-eez): Calories are measurements of energy found in food. Kids need calories to play sports and to do well in school.

diabetes (di-a-BEET-eez): Diabetes is a condition where the body is not able to control how it uses sugar. If someone is obese, he or she may be at risk of getting type 2 diabetes.

fat (fat): Fat is one part of food that provides and stores energy for the body. Fat helps the body use some of the vitamins found in food.

heart disease (hart di-ZEEZ): Heart disease is a word used to describe a number of heart conditions. Heart disease can affect your heart and your blood vessels.

minerals (MIN-er-ulz): Minerals are elements—such as calcium, magnesium, and iron—that are needed for the body to function and are found in food. People get their daily minerals from fruits, vegetables, protein, grains, and dairy foods.

nutrients (NOO-tree-ents): Nutrients are substances the body needs to grow. Vitamins and minerals are nutrients.

obese (oh-BEES): An obese person is very overweight. Being obese can cause health problems and self-esteem issues.

overweight (OH-ver-wayt): People who are overweight weigh more and have more fat than they should for their heights. Being overweight can lead to obesity.

protein (PRO-teen): Protein is a part of food that provides energy and contains building blocks used by the whole body. Proteins are found in meat, nuts, and seeds.

self-esteem (self e-STEEM): Self-esteem is having respect for yourself and your skills. Being a healthy weight can improve your self-esteem.

vitamins (VYE-tuh-minz): A vitamin is a substance found in foods and is something that our bodies need to function properly. Fruits and vegetables are a good source of vitamins.

To Learn More

BOOKS

Greene, Tiger. *Sacking Obesity: The Team Tiger Game Plan for Kids Who Want to Lose Weight, Feel Great, and Win on and off the Playing Field*. New York: HarperOne, 2012.

Zinczenko, David and Matt Goulding. *Eat This, Not That! for Kids!: Be the Leanest, Fittest Family on the Block!* Emmaus, PA: Rodale, 2008.

WEB SITES

Visit our Web site for links about obesity: **childsworld.com/links**

Note to Parents, Teachers, and Librarians: We routinely verify our Web links to make sure they are safe and active sites. So encourage your readers to check them out!

Index